D1686040

GALE

CENGAGE Learning

Novels for Students, Volume 40

Project Editor: Sara Constantakis **Rights Acquisition and Management**: Leitha Etheridge-Sims, Tracie Richardson **Composition**: Evi Abou-El-Seoud **Manufacturing**: Rhonda Dover

Imaging: John Watkins

Product Design: Pamela A. E. Galbreath, Jennifer Wahi **Content Conversion**: Katrina Coach **Product Manager**: Meggin Condino © 2012 Gale, Cengage Learning

Gale
27500 Drake Rd.
Farmington Hills, MI, 48331-3535

ISBN-13: 978-1-4144-8538-6
ISBN-10: 1-4144-8538-7
ISSN 1094-3552

This title is also available as an e-book.

ISBN-13: 978-1-4144-8231-6
ISBN-10: 1-4144-8231-0
Contact your Gale, a part of Cengage Learning sales
representative for ordering information.

Printed in Mexico
1 2 3 4 5 6 7 16 15 14 13 12

White Teeth

Zadie Smith

2000

Introduction

White Teeth is Zadie Smith's first novel, published in 2000 when she was only twenty-four years old. *White Teeth* burst upon the literary scene with great fanfare. The book was an international bestseller and won the Whitbread First Novel Award, the London *Guardian's* First Book Award, the James Tait Black Memorial Prize for Fiction, and the Commonwealth Writers' First Book Award. When *White Teeth* was published, it seemed to be like no other novel being written at the time, especially as a novel written by someone so young. It has been lauded for its comic energy, for its Dickensian characters, and for its inventive storytelling, as well as for the appeal it holds for readers of many generations and from all kinds of backgrounds.

White Teeth follows the lives of two British World War II veterans, Archie Jones and Samad Iqbal. Archie is a modest Englishman who marries a beautiful Jamaican woman and just wants to get along. Samad is a bombastic Bengali Muslim who marries a much younger Bengali woman and chafes at his ignominious life as a waiter. The two friends have children at the same time. Archie and Clara Jones have a girl, Irie, while Samad and Alsana Iqbal give birth to twin boys, Magid and Millat. As the children grow up in the multicultural swirl of London, their parents must confront the realities of assimilation. As teenagers, these three are mentored by the Chalfens, an aspirational middle-class family, which causes consternation among their parents. *White Teeth* is, at heart, a meditation on immigration and exile, the contradictory longings for freedom and connection.

It should be stressed that *White Teeth* is not appropriate for younger readers as it covers adult themes and includes descriptions of adult sexuality and some violence. It also uses the frank slang of North London, including adult curse words.

Author Biography

Smith was born Sadie Smith on October 25, 1975, in London, England, and grew up in Willesden Green, where she would later set *White Teeth*. Her mother, Yvonne Bailey, immigrated from Jamaica in 1969, and she became Harvey Smith's second wife. They divorced when Smith was a teenager, and she has two older half-siblings and two younger brothers. In an interview published in *BoldType*, Random House's online magazine, Smith noted that

> from the age of five to fifteen, I really wanted to be a musical movie actress. I tap danced for ten years before I began to understand people don't make musicals anymore.... Slowly but surely the pen became mightier than the double pick-up timestep with shuffle.

At fourteen, Smith changed her first name from Sadie to Zadie. Although she admits she was not a dedicated student in secondary school, she nonetheless gained admission to the prestigious Cambridge University.

She studied English literature at Cambridge, which is where she began writing *White Teeth*. In the same interview in *BoldType*, she said that

> The novel began as a short story

which expanded. It was a natural enough thing to happen.... I was walking into novella territory which is no good, so when I got to eighty pages, and after the encouragement of a few people, I just kept going.

The reception of the first one hundred pages of *White Teeth* is legendary in literary circles. Taken up by the prestigious Andrew Wylie agency, the pages sparked an auction, with publishing rights eventually being sold to Hamish Hamilton, the U.K. imprint of Penguin Books, for a reputed 250,000 pounds sterling (about $400,000 at the time). Smith's editor, Simon Prosser, told Maria Russo of *Salon* that "It's very rare for 100 pages to be greeted with this much excitement. What we saw was this work that appealed to anyone, regardless of age, gender or political position." *White Teeth* became an international bestseller, for which Smith won a variety of prestigious awards, including three recognizing its merits as a first novel.

Smith has published two subsequent novels, *The Autograph Man* (2002) and *On Beauty* (2005), for which she won the Orange Prize and was shortlisted for the Man Booker Prize. In 2009, she published *Changing My Mind*, a collection of occasional essays on writing, movies, literature, and other subjects. Smith has taught at Harvard and Columbia universities, and in 2010, she joined the creative writing faculty at New York University. In 2004 she married the poet and novelist Nick Laird, whom she met at Cambridge, and in 2009, they had a daughter named Katherine.

Plot Summary

Part One: Archie 1974, 1945

CHAPTER 1: THE PECULIAR SECOND MARRIAGE OF ARCHIE JONES

Archibald Jones decides to kill himself on New Year's Day 1975, but he is interrupted by Mo Hussein-Ishmael, who runs him off. Archie is in despair because his wife both is mad and has divorced him, and because he is middle-aged and disappointed. After failing to kill himself, he drives around town, filled with joy that he is not dead, and comes across a house with a huge sign out front, "Welcome to the 'End of the World' Party 1975." Archie invites himself into the house in which a number of young people are living, and after drinking with several of them and arguing about the war, he meets and falls instantly in love with Clara Bowden.

CHAPTER 2: TEETHING TROUBLE

Chapter 2 tells how Clara Bowden came to be in that squat on New Year's morning where she met Archie Jones. Clara was seeing Ryan Topps, a redheaded, freckled fellow who is considered the least datable boy in school. Ryan is rebellious, rides a scooter, and occasionally buys drugs from the inhabitants of the squat in which Clara meets Archie. Clara is horrified when she comes home from school to find her mother and Ryan deep in conversation, and as Hortense convinces Ryan that the end of the world is coming, Clara loses interest in him. Ryan proceeds to crash the Vespa into a tree, resulting in Clara's lost front teeth. And so, that morning in the squat, when Clara sees Archie, she transfers the longing for a savior inculcated by her religious childhood onto the unlikely figure of Archie Jones.

CHAPTER 3: TWO FAMILIES

Archie and Clara wed at the registry office with only Samad and Alsana as their witnesses and move to a house in Willesden Green, a suburb of London. Hortense disowns Clara because Archie is white. Samad and Alsana live nearby, although their own move has been a strain on their finances. Samad is not a very good waiter, and as a result he makes bad tips, incurring the scorn of his fellow employees and giving his employer an excuse to deny him a raise when he asks. Pregnant Alsana has a fight with her husband when he tells her this, then walks to town, where she picks up his repaired shoes from the cobbler. On the return trip, she passes Clara in her front yard, and the two women bond over the realization that although their husbands tell one another everything, they tell their wives nothing.

Media Adaptations

- *White Teeth* is available as an unabridged audiobook published by Recorded Books in 2001. It is available on various Web sites.

- The British Broadcasting Corporation produced a four-episode television series, *White Teeth*, in 2002. It aired in the United States on the Public Broadcasting System's *Masterpiece Theater* in 2003. It is not available on VHS or DVD but can be streamed online at Hulu.com.

CHAPTER 4: THREE COMING

Archie greets the news that Clara is pregnant with great joy. As Archie is celebrating, his boss, Kelvin Hero, calls him upstairs. Despite Hero's best efforts, Archie never does understand that his coworkers and the firm's customers are scandalized by his interracial marriage, and Hero buys him off with a stack of free lunch vouchers. Alsana is also pregnant, with twins, and as their pregnancies proceed, she and Clara become increasingly close friends. Neena, Alsana's niece, is scandalized by Alsana's arranged marriage. Sitting on a park bench, Neena tries to convince Alsana that a good marriage requires true communication between spouses, while Alsana argues with equal vehemence that "silence, what is not said, is the very best recipe for family life."

CHAPTER 5: THE ROOT CANALS OF ALFRED ARCHIBALD JONES AND SAMAD MIAH

This chapter relates the history of Archie and Samad's experiences in World War II. Assigned to the same tank crew, they served with three other men, Roy Mackintosh, Will Johnson, and Captain Thomas Dickinson-Smith. Their tank breaks down, and while Samad and Archie are in the village having drinks, the other three men are killed. The war ends, but no one tells them, and they take refuge in an abandoned hospital, where Samad discovers the joys of powdered morphine. To pass the time, Samad tells Archie about his great-grandfather Mangal Pande, the Indian mutineer. Eventually, a group of Russian soldiers arrives with orders to capture Dr. Perret, the man known as "Dr. Sick," who is a Nazi scientist. Afterward, Samad bullies Archie into killing the Frenchman. Archie takes him into the woods, a shot is heard, and Archie returns to the car, bleeding from a wound.

Part Two: Samad 1984, 1857

CHAPTER 6: THE TEMPTATION OF SAMAD IQBAL

This chapter takes place in 1984, when the two couples' children, Magid, Millat, and Irie, are nine years old. Samad becomes active in the children's school and protests the upcoming Harvest Festival. After the meeting, Poppy Burt-Jones, the childrens' music teacher, approaches Samad, and he finds himself falling hopelessly in lust with her. For the next several weeks Samad is afflicted with a case of desire so severe that he is nearly hobbled by a constant need to relieve himself. As a devout Muslim, self-pleasure is forbidden, and Samad attempts to fast in order to assuage his religious guilt. Finally, he meets with Poppy Burt-Jones, and they end the meeting by kissing passionately.

CHAPTER 7: MOLARS

On the day that Millat, Magid, and Irie travel across London to deliver Harvest Festival canned goods to Mr. J. P. Hamilton, Samad packs a bag and prepares to meet Poppy Burt-Jones. The children descend on Mr. J. P. Hamilton, who first tries to shoo them away, then invites them inside, only to insult them with racist stories while lecturing them on the importance of dental hygiene. The children flee, while Samad fends off an attack by Mad Mary on himself and Poppy Burt-Jones. As Samad and Poppy sit on a bench to discuss the moral implications of their impending affair, Samad looks up to see his sons waving at him from the park gazebo.

CHAPTER 8: MITOSIS

Named for the biological process of cell division that causes a single cell to split into two identical copies, this chapter follows Samad as he decides to split up his twins and send one back to Bangladesh. Samad is reeling from the sense of damnation he believes he has incurred through his affair with Poppy Burt-Jones. Convening with Archie in O'Connell's, Samad confesses all, including that he feels he has damned his children. At first, he determines to send both boys back to Bangladesh, but he can only afford to send one. Knowing that Alsana will never agree, he hatches a secret plan to kidnap one son. Samad cuts off relations with Poppy, who shows up as a customer at the restaurant on the very night Archie is to meet him after his shift with Magid, the twin he has finally decided upon. Archie arrives with all three children in the car, and Archie lies, saying that Magid is merely going on holiday.

CHAPTER 9: MUTINY!

Alsana believes that people who have grown up under the threat of imminent physical disaster hold life lightly, and it is Samad's sending Magid to a part of the world where he is at the mercy of this that forms the core of Alsana's anger at him. In revenge, Alsana begins answering Samad's every question with a question in order to "force him to live like she did—never knowing, never being sure." Meanwhile, Millat becomes exactly what his father feared, "a rudeboy, a badman, at the forefront, changing image as often as shoes." Millat idolizes movie gangsters, and as he grows into his "fierce good looks," he begins a precocious career as a ladies' man. Millat and his crew travel to Bradford to protest the publication of a book considered anti-Muslim. Alsana sees Millat on the television, and to teach him a lesson, she burns all of his pop-culture artifacts: books, movies, posters, sneakers, clothing. The night the Berlin Wall falls, the Joneses are at the Iqbal house, watching it on television.

CHAPTER 10: THE ROOT CANALS OF MANGAL PANDE

Samad and Archie ring in the 1990s in O'Connell's, a place they love for its unchanging nature. Samad has brought the portrait of his great-grandfather Mangal Pande, which he finally persuaded Abdul-Mickey to hang on the wall. Samad insists on the heroic nature of his ancestor, but all that winter he and Archie argue, as Archie accrues evidence from the historic record that has rendered *Pande* synonymous with "coward" or "traitor." When Archie argues that the truth depends on the source, Samad disagrees, imploring of his friend, "Please, let us not get into the nature of truth." Archie floats a theory that Mangal Pande deliberately missed his crucial shot because his friends had put him up to starting the mutiny, but he did not want to actually kill a man. Samad argues that this cannot be true, that a real man will always rise to the occasion. Archie answers, "And there will be people he will save."

Part Three: Irie 1990, 1907

CHAPTER 11: THE MISEDUCATION OF IRIE JONES

Irie Jones has been miseducated about many things including the size of her body, the nature of her hair, and the meaning of Shakespeare's Sonnet 127. Irie at fifteen has inherited her grandmother's "substantial Jamaican frame" and a huge fluffy Afro. She goes to P.K.'s Afro Hair, where the hairdresser burns her hair off, then offers to put in a free weave to make up for it. Crowned with "a full head of long, straight, reddish-black hair" she heads straight to the Iqbal house, where she is convinced that if Millat could only see her, he would fall in love with her. Neena is there with her girlfriend, and the two are horrified by what she has done. Irie, Millat, and Joshua Chalfen get caught with a marijuana cigarette during a drug raid, and the three of them are sentenced to two months of after-school study at Joshua's house.

CHAPTER 12: CANINES, THE RIPPING TEETH

The Chalfens are people who thrive on changing others, first their own children and then

Irie and Millat. Irie is entranced by their household, where conversation flowed "freely from adult to child, child to adult." Millat entrances Joyce Chalfen, who is smitten with his beauty. Clara and Alsana become increasingly concerned as their children are subsumed into the Chalfen household. Alsana claims that "these people are taking my son away from me! … They're Englishifying him completely!" Irie claims to feel her brain changing "from something mushy to something hard and defined." Alsana sends Neena to check the Chalfens out, and her lesbianism so rattles Joyce that Neena reports back that the Chalfens are completely insane. Finally Clara goes to meet Joyce, where she is met with unthinking racism.

CHAPTER 13: THE ROOT CANALS OF HORTENSE BOWDEN

Like all the "root canal" chapters, this one tells a family history, in this case how Hortense Bowden came to be born during the Jamaican earthquake of 1907. Hortense's mother, Ambrosia, is a pretty teenage girl when she catches the eye of Captain Charlie Durham, who rapes her, conceiving Hortense, and begins an affair with her. Ambrosia is five months pregnant when Captain Durham disappears. She is sent to Mrs. Brenton, who "specialized in lost souls." Mrs. Brenton introduces the Bowden clan to the Jehovah's Witnesses. When Ambrosia is nearly at term, Sir Glenard leads her into the church of St. Antonia, where he attempts to rape her. The earthquake hits, and he is killed. Ambrosia gives birth to Hortense on her own.

Durham returns and tries to find Ambrosia to take her to England, but his superior says there is no room on the boats "for black whores or livestock."

CHAPTER 14: MORE ENGLISH THAN THE ENGLISH

Marcus Chalfen, Josh Chalfen's father and a geneticist working with mice, begins corresponding with Magid several times a week. Irie, who is in charge of organizing Marcus's papers, is not above borrowing them. Thus she learns that Marcus thinks that her intelligence is second-rate but that she might make a good dentist. Although hurt, Irie decides to pursue the idea. Meanwhile KEVIN, the Keepers of the Eternal and Victorious Islamic Nation, the group to which Millat belongs, pressures him to drop his only real girlfriend, Karina Cain, because she is English. Millat brushes them off, but eventually he breaks up with her, then repairs to the Chalfen house, where Joyce is waiting in the kitchen with tea and advice. Irie discovers that Clara has false teeth. In a fit of adolescent betrayal and pique, she packs up her things and moves to her grandmother's house.

CHAPTER 15: CHALFENISM VERSUS BOWDENISM

Irie is surprised to find Ryan Topps living in her grandmother's spare room, while Irie's resemblance to Clara is as big a surprise to Ryan Topps. Ryan has become an elder in the Jehovah's Witnesses and a dedicated help to Hortense. Irie dreams about escaping to what she imagines is "a place where things simply were. No fictions, no myths, no lies, no tangled webs." Joshua Chalfen comes to visit her at Hortense's, filled with zeal about animal rights and certain his parents are hypocrites. Samad also comes to visit her, heartbroken that Millat has become "a green-bow-tie-wearing terrorist" while Magid is a "pukka Englishman." Ryan Topps receives word from Brooklyn that the world will end in the year 2000, and Hortense, determined to live to see the day, tells Irie she'll take her to Jamaica for the event.

Part Four: Magid, Millat, and Marcus 1992, 1999

CHAPTER 16: THE RETURN OF MAGID MAHFOOZ MURSHED MUBTASIM IQBAL

While waiting for Magid's plane, Marcus gets into a conversation with an Anglo-Indian girl who has read his book and finds it alarming. Since the book's publication, Marcus has been bewildered by the reaction from nonscientists. When Magid's return causes Millat to threaten to move out, Magid goes to live with the Chalfens, where he becomes Marcus's right-hand man. Irie realizes that Magid, like Mad Mary and the other street prophets, has the light of prophecy in his eyes. Joyce decides that the boys' problems are not prophecy but trauma. Irie tells her to butt out and to pay more attention to her own children, but Joyce cannot be deterred.

CHAPTER 17: CRISIS TALKS AND

ELEVENTH-HOUR TACTICS

Joyce takes it upon herself to visit Alsana in order to arrange a meeting between Millat and Magid. The two women argue over whose fault the boys' estrangement is, and Millat could not be more pleased to be the center of both women's attention. Samad takes Magid to O'Connell's, where Magid orders a bacon sandwich, engendering Samad's wrath. Irie is pressed into service to deliver the key to the neutral room in the university where the two boys are to meet, and when she touches Millat, he kisses her, and they wind up having sex. Horrified and embarrassed, Irie, seeking someone to blame for the fact that Millat will not love her, goes back to the Chalfens', where she seduces Magid. The brothers meet, agree to disagree, and then argue about every slight between them for hours without ever coming to an agreement.

CHAPTER 18: THE END OF HISTORY VERSUS THE LAST MAN

Millat and KEVIN, led by Brother Ibrahim ad-Din Shukrallah, plan to stop Marcus, arguing that man should not presume to create, that creation is solely the province of Allah. Joshua has joined FATE—Fighting Animal Torture and Exploitation —a group that opposes FutureMouse on animal rights grounds, and they debate whether to attack Marcus himself or to try to free the FutureMouse. Josh argues that freeing FutureMouse is absurd, since its fate is coded into its genes by Marcus. Hortense and Ryan Topps call Irie to tell her they will be there, protesting on similar grounds to those cited by KEVIN. And Magid is thrilled to be assisting Marcus through every stage of creating the FutureMouse, a creature for whom there is "No second-guessing, no what-ifs, no might-have-beens."

CHAPTER 19: THE FINAL SPACE

As the English begin their New Years' revels, the members of FATE, KEVIN, the Jehovah's Witnesses, and the Iqbal and Jones clans travel across London to the FutureMouse launch. Josh is very stoned, in part because he feels there is nothing he can do at this point to stop either his father's work in genetics or the FATE crew's determination to interrupt it. Millat is also deeply stoned, and when the seven members of KEVIN get to Trafalgar Square, Millat breaks off from them to contemplate the difference between the name his father scrawled under a park bench when he first came to England and the statue of the English governor who executed his ancestor Mangal Pande. Ryan Topps on his scooter, with Hortense in the sidecar, leads a bus full of Witnesses into London. The Iqbal and Jones families are squabbling as usual on the bus into town when Irie, pregnant, launches into a soliloquy about the futility of their obsessions with the past.

CHAPTER 20: OF MICE AND MEMORY

Archie chats with Abdul-Mickey about the potential for Marcus's genetic research to cure the hereditary skin condition from which all of Mickey's family suffers. Josh wonders whether his father, the rational Chalfenist, will agree to sacrifice FutureMouse to save his son from Crispin's gun. Millat fingers the gun in his pocket and muses on his mutinous ancestor Mangal Pande. Irie wonders which brother is the father of her child. Samad leaves to confront Hortense and her Witnesses, to ask them to keep it down, but finds he agrees with them. Marcus introduces his mentor, who turns out to be Dr. Perret, just as Samad reenters the room and learns that Archie did not kill Dr. Perret in the woods after all. Archie sees Millat acting strangely and lunges to prevent him from shooting, taking a shot in the thigh and crashing through the glass case, setting the FutureMouse free. In the aftermath, since none of the Jones or Iqbal families will testify, the judge sentences both Millat and Magid to community service with Joyce Chalfant. Meanwhile, Joshua Chalfant and Irie fall in love and end up in Jamaica with Hortense and Irie's little girl, frolicking in the surf and greeting the turn of the millennium.

Characters

White Teeth is famous for the number and variety of characters Smith included. Seeming to emulate Charles Dickens, she gave even minor characters full names and physical descriptions. In the interest of clarity, this section describes only those characters who are mentioned in the plot summary or who otherwise have a material effect on the plot of the novel.

Abdul-Mickey

Abdul-Mickey, also known as Mickey, is the owner and short-order cook at O'Connell's Irish Poolroom, an establishment that is neither Irish nor a poolroom and to which Archie and Samad retire each evening. Mickey suffers from a stupendous and genetic acne situation, and he refuses to cook or serve pork in his pub.

Shiva Bhagwati

Shiva Bhagwati is the only Hindu waiter at the Palace Restaurant where Samad works. In the beginning of the novel, he is young and handsome and collects the most tips of any of the waiters, a situation he uses against Samad, since Samad gets terrible tips and contributes little to the pool that must be divided equally every night. Over time, he becomes a confidante of Samad's, especially during the Poppy Burt-Jones episode, when he warns Samad that relations with English girls never work out because there is "too much bloody history." Later he becomes deeply involved in KEVIN.

Ambrosia Bowden

Ambrosia Bowden is the mother of Hortense. She was raped as a teenager by Captain Charlie Durham, thus conceiving Hortense, to whom she gives birth in the middle of the 1907 earthquake.

Darcus Bowden

Darcus Bowden is the husband of Hortense and father of Clara. He emigrated from Jamaica in 1961.

Hortense Bowden

Hortense is the mother of Clara, grandmother of Irie. She was born in the middle of the 1907 earthquake. A dedicated member of the Jehovah's Witnesses, she followed her husband from Jamaica to England in 1972. In her old age, she takes in Ryan Topps as a boarder and helpmeet, and they continue to work for the Witnesses.

Mrs. Brenton

Mrs. Brenton is the Scottish widow with whom Ambrosia Bowden is sent to live during the last months of her pregnancy. She introduces the

Bowden clan to the Jehovah's Witnesses.

Poppy Burt-Jones

Poppy Burt-Jones teaches orchestra to the Iqbal twins and has an affair with Samad. She is young, in her late twenties, thin and freckled, with dark red hair.

Karina Cain

Karina is the one girlfriend Millat really likes, but because she is white, the members of KEVIN convince Millat that the relationship is inappropriate, and he breaks up with her.

Benjamin Chalfen

Benjamin is the second Chalfen son. He wants to be a geneticist like his father when he grows up.

Jack Chalfen

Jack Chalfen is the third Chalfen son. He wants to be a psychiatrist when he grows up.

Joshua Chalfen

Joshua Chalfen is the oldest Chalfen son. He attends the Glenard Oak School along with Irie and Millat. They meet during the drug raid that Samad instigates as head of the Parent-Teacher Association, following which Joshua is sentenced to tutor Millat and Irie after school for two months. As a teenager he joins FATE, an animal rights organization opposed to Marcus's work. As adults, he and Irie become a couple.

Joyce Chalfen

Joyce Chalfen is the mother of Joshua, Benjamin, Jack, and Oscar and the wife of Marcus. She is a garden writer and a dedicated mother of the middle-class variety. She thrives on fixing other people, first her family and then Irie and Millat. She is struck by Millat's beauty and listens to his problems and gives him money. She prides herself on the happiness of her marriage, the genius of her husband and her children, and her own sexiness.

Marcus Chalfen

Marcus Chalfen is the father of Joshua and his brothers and husband to Joyce. He is a geneticist who creates "mice whose very bodies did exactly what Marcus told them." Marcus believes in the "perfectibility of all life, in the possibility of making it more efficient, more logical."

Oscar Chalfen

Oscar is the youngest of the Chalfen children.

Clarence

Clarence is an elderly Jamaican man who

frequents O'Connell's pub with Denzel.

Crispin

Crispin and his wife, Joely, founded FATE, Fighting Animal Torture and Exploitation, the organization that opposes Marcus Chalfen's FutureMouse experiment.

Denzel

Denzel is an elderly Jamaican man who frequents O'Connell's pub with Clarence.

Thomas Dickinson-Smith

Thomas Dickinson-Smith is the captain of the tank in which Archie and Samad met during World War II. He thinks his homosexuality is a secret, but his men all sense it and loathe him for it. To hide his lust for Samad, he picks on him and encourages the men in calling Samad "Sultan." He dies by his own hand when the tank is attacked after breaking down. Unbeknownst to any of them, it is on that very day that an end is declared to the war in Europe.

Captain Charlie Durham

Captain Charlie Durham rapes Ambrosia Bowden, thereby conceiving Hortense. For several months after this event he tutors Ambrosia, but then he abandons her abruptly.

Sir Edmund Fletcher Glenard

Sir Edmund Fletcher Glenard is an Englishman who made a fortune in Jamaica. He founded the workhouse that became the Glenard Oak School that Irie, Joshua, and Millat attend. He died while trying to rape Irie's grandmother during the Jamaican earthquake of 1907.

Mr. J. P. Hamilton

Mr. J. P. Hamilton is a prejudiced old white man to whom Irie, Magrid, and Millat deliver food collected during the Harvest Festival. He lectures them on the care of their teeth and angers Millat when he declares that his father could not have served in the army because "there were certainly no wogs as I remember."

Kelvin Hero

Hero is Archie's boss at MorganHero Direct Mail Specialists. His unsuccessful attempt to tell Archie that his coworkers are uncomfortable with the biracial marriage he has made falls on deaf ears. In order to placate his own guilty conscience, he gives Archie a stack of lunch vouchers.

Arshad Hussein-Ishmael

Arshad Hussein-Ishmael is the son of Mo Hussein-Ishmael, who discovers Archie trying to gas himself to death in his car.

Mo Hussein-Ishmael

Mo Husein-Ishmael owns a butcher shop. He prevents Archie from killing himself. He is also Ardashir Mukhul's brother-in-law, and late in the book he joins KEVIN.

Horst Ibelgaufts

Horst is a Swedish gynecologist who tied for thirteenth place with Archie Jones in the London Olympics of 1948. Horst keeps in touch by sending gnomic letters over the years, each of which seems to arrive just as Archie is in desperate need of advice.

Alsana Begum Iqbal

Alsana is the wife of Samad and mother of the twins Magid and Millat. She is a Bengali Muslim who married Samad when she was just twenty and came with him to England. Alsana earns a living sewing garments for a sex shop in Soho called Domination. After Samad sends Magid away, Alsana only speaks to Samad in questions for the next eight years.

Magid Mahfooz Murshed Mubtasim Iqbal

Magid Iqbal is the elder twin son of Alsana and Samad. Magid is the intellectual one of the twins, displaying from an early age a bookish nature and an impressive command of science. He is caught at age nine pretending to be "Mark Smith," an alter ego he invented in order to fit in with the other English children.

Millat Zulfikar Iqbal

Millat Iqbal is the younger twin son of Alsana and Samad. Millat is the beautiful twin, the one who gets by on his looks and charm. He becomes deeply involved in KEVIN, the Keepers of the Eternal and Victorious Islamic Nation, although his deepest desire is to become a gangster. Irie has a crush on him through their entire childhood, but until that fateful afternoon just before the launch of FutureMouse, he refuses her attentions because she is the only person who really knows him.

Samad Miah Iqbal

Samad is the husband of Alsana, father of the twins Magid and Millat, and best friend to Archie Jones. He is a Bengali Muslim who works as a waiter in an Indian restaurant. Due to an accident in the trenches at the beginning of the war in which Samad was accidentally shot through his wrist, his right hand hangs dead at his side. Samad came to England in 1973 seeking a better life. Samad and Archie spend every evening in O'Connell's together and remain lifelong friends.

Joely

Joely and her husband Crispin founded FATE, Fighting Animal Torture and Exploitation, the organization that opposes Marcus Chalfen's FutureMouse experiment. Joshua is in love with Joely, as are most of the young men in the group.

Will Johnson

Will Johnson is the gunner of the tank in which Archie and Samad met during World War II. He is considered a "bit simple." He is strangled with a cheese wire when the tank breaks down and Archie and Samad have walked into town for a drink. Unbeknownst to any of them, it is on that very day that an end is declared to the war in Europe.

Alfred Archibald Jones

Archie is the father of Irie, husband first of Ophelia, then of Clara Bowden, and best friend to Samad Iqbal. Archie was seventeen when he joined the army in World War II and fought with Samad in Italy. Although he wanted to be a journalist, he wound up working for a direct mail company designing folded documents. He participated as a cyclist in the London Olympics of 1948, where he shared thirteenth place with Horst Ibelgaufts, but he was omitted from the records. Archie did not kill Dr. Perret in the woods at the end of the war, and he saves him and Marcus from Millat's gunfire at the end of the novel.

Clara Bowden Jones

Clara is Archie's second wife, the mother of Irie and the daughter of Hortense. She is a black Jamaican who emigrated to England at age sixteen. She is raised a strict Jehovah's Witness by her mother, Hortense, who disowns her when she marries Archie. When she meets Archie, she is nineteen and missing her two front teeth, but to him she is the most beautiful and comforting creature he has ever seen. She returns to college when Irie is a schoolgirl and opposes Irie's return to Hortense's house.

Irie Ambrosia Jones

Irie Jones is the daughter of Archie and Clara Jones. She and Millat and Magid Iqbal are all born within weeks of one another and grow up nearly like siblings. Irie is in love with each of the brothers at different times, especially as she grows into an awkward teenager. She decides to go into dentistry after reading in a letter from Marcus Chalfen to Magid Iqbal that Marcus thinks she is not quite bright enough for the hard sciences. She sleeps with both Iqbal boys and becomes pregnant but never knows which one is the father. She eventually partners with Joshua Chalfen, and they raise her daughter together.

Ophelia Diagilo Jones

Ophelia Jones is Archie's first wife, who

divorces him at the beginning of the novel. She is "a violet-eyed Italian with a faint mustache." They met in Italy just after the war, and she went mad upon their return to England and believes that she is "the maid of the fifteenth-century art lover Cosimo de'Medici."

Roy Mackintosh

Roy Mackintosh is the co-driver of the tank in which Archie and Samad met during World War II. He dislikes Samad and nicknames him "Sultan." He is shot in the back by unknown assailants when the tank breaks down and Archie and Samad have walked into town for a drink. Unbeknownst to any of them, it is on that very day that an end is declared to the war in Europe.

Hakim and Zinat Mahal

Hakim is Samad's cousin. He and his wife, Zinat, run a discount store in Poppy Burt-Jones's neighborhood, where Samad visits them before his assignation with her in order to establish an alibi. It is Zinat who helps Samad kidnap Magid and flies with him to Bangladesh.

Mad Mary

Mad Mary is a street person who haunts Harlesden and accosts Samad and Poppy on their first outing together.

Maxine

Maxine is Neena's girlfriend. She is "a sexy and slender girl … with a beautiful porcelain face, dark eyes, and a lot of curly brown hair." She tells Irie to stop following Magid around and lectures her on her own beauty.

Merlin

See Tim Westleigh

Ardashir Mukhul

Ardashir Mukhul is Samad's distant cousin and his employer at the Palace Restaurant.

Neena

Although Neena is Alsana's niece, she is only two years younger than Alsana. Alsana calls her "niece of shame" because she has lesbian relationships, but they are actually quite close.

Mangal Pande

Mangal Pande was an actual Indian whose attack against his commanding officers was an instigating factor in what came to be known as the Sepoy Rebellion against British colonial rule. He lived from 1827 to 1857, and the Indian government issued a stamp with his picture in 1984. Pande was executed in 1857 for attacking his superiors, and this action, in conjunction with the widespread rumor among Indian troops that bullet cartridges, which they were obligated to bite in order to open, were greased with beef or pork fat, each of which was a violation of Hindu or Muslim dietary regulations, set off the rebellion. Samad Iqbal claims Pande as his great-grandfather and often refers to his glory, usually to the incomprehension of his listeners.

Dr. Marc-Pierre Perret

Dr. Marc-Pierre Perret is called "Dr. Sick" by the local Bulgarian children in the village where Samad and Archie end the war. The Russians inform the two Englishmen that the doctor is in fact a dangerous Nazi and that they have orders to kill him. He suffers from diabetic reinopathy, which causes his eyes to excrete blood. Samad thought that Archie had killed the doctor in the woods during the war, but in fact, the doctor shot Archie. Later, he became Marcus Chalfen's mentor and a major investor in FutureMouse. Archie saves Perret and Marcus when Millat tries to shoot them.

Nickolai Pesotsky

Nickolai Pesotsky is the Russian soldier who informs Samad and Archie that not only is the war over, but the fellow they have known as "Dr. Sick" is actually a dangerous Nazi. Pesotsky has a glass eye that he takes out to show off to the two Englishmen.

Brother Ibrahim ad-Din Shukrallah

Brother Ibrahim is the founder of KEVIN, the Keepers of the Eternal and Victorious Islamic Nation. Born Monty Clyde Benjamin in Barbados in 1960, he converted to Islam and then studied in Saudi Arabia for five years before his radical ideas became problematic. He came to England and spent five more years locked in his aunt's garage, studying and doing exercises, before announcing himself a prophet who would unite politics and religion in the Asian and black communities. Brother Ibrahim advocates violent action, for which the mainstream Islamic community ostracizes him.

Ryan Topps

Ryan Topps was originally Clara Bowden's teenage boyfriend. He is "very thin and very tall, redheaded, flat-footed, and freckled to such an extent that his skin was rarer than his freckles." He rides a Vespa scooter and is considered by Clara's schoolmates the person they would not date even if he were the last man on earth. Decades later he becomes the roommate and companion to Clara's mother, Hortense, and an elder in the Jehovah's Witnesses.

Tim Westleigh

Tim Westleigh is the host of Clara Bowden's failed "Welcome to the 'End of the World' Party," and it is at his house that Archie meets Clara for the first time.

Themes

History

The characters in *White Teeth* are haunted by history. History is what brought this divergent set of characters, the Jones, Iqbal, and Chalfen families, to Willesden Green, and it is over the meaning of historical events that they argue and even plot violence against one another. Smith's characters are formed by history. They fight with one another about the meaning of history and attempt to control the forward march of history, but ultimately they are all equally enmeshed in the historical, political, social, and familial networks in which they live.

Topics for Further Study

- Ethnic heritage is a central theme in

White Teeth, and the characters have very different attitudes about assimilation and cultural identity. Interview your parents and grandparents about your own ethnic background. Where did your family originate? How long ago did they immigrate to America? Is ethnic identity important to your family, and if so, how is that ethnic identity maintained? Build a Web site whose elements include video interviews with your family, visual representations of their immigration story, recordings of traditional performers, and links to research about ethnic organizations working to keep those traditions alive.

- The critic James Wood declared in a review in the *New Republic* that *White Teeth* is representative of a new literary genre, one he named "hysterical realism." Research Wood's critical take on the novel, and write a paper in which you argue for or against his definition. Do you agree with him? Do you disagree with him? Why? Use specific examples from the novel.

- Food is a marker of both class and identity in *White Teeth*. Note the different foods eaten by the Jones,

Bowden, Iqbal, and Chalfen families, as well as the food rules that Abdul-Mickey enforces at O'Connell's. Interview your parents, grandparents, aunts, or uncles and ask them to tell you about a family dish. Then ask them to teach you how to cook their favorite family dish. Write up a recipe for this dish, complete with ingredients, measurements, and instructions. Pretend you are producing a cooking show, and create a video presentation that explains the origins of your family dish and that can be used to teach someone else how to make it.

- Gene Luen Yang's prizewinning graphic novel for young adults *American Born Chinese* (2008) is the story of Jin Wang, a lonely Taiwanese American boy navigating the challenges of middle school in San Francisco. The novel filters Jin Wang's feelings of being born in the wrong body through the story of a Chinese folk hero, the Monkey King, and through the figure of Chin-kee, an amalgamation of every ugly Chinese American stereotype. Imagine an encounter between Jin Wang and Irie, Millat, and Magid, and tell the story of that encounter in a graphic story of your own. The story should have a beginning, a middle, and an end, and something significant needs to occur between these characters.

- Marcus Chalfen's life work involves splicing genes across species. Research this topic. What is the current state of trans-species genetic experimentation? Are there laws in the United States that govern such research? To what purpose is such research being conducted? Are there groups who oppose this research? Have they resorted to violence against researchers? Prepare a presentation for your class that traces the current state of such research and that analyzes whether or not the FutureMouse is a realistic example of genetic research and the opposition it engenders.

- Zadie Smith's essay "Dead Man Walking" is about her love of English comedy, a love she shared with her father. Read the essay, and research comedy as a genre, the English comic tradition in particular. Get together with several classmates, and using at least one character from *White Teeth* as a starting point for each sketch, write three comedy

sketches in the English tradition.
Perform them for your class.

John Mullan, writing in the London *Guardian*, notes the manner in which Smith "incorporates in her novel two different kinds of historical time that have usually been found in two different species of the English novel. First, there is what might be called 'recent history.'" Mullan notes, "We begin in 1974 and approach the time of the book's composition through episodes in the 1980s and early 90s." He then outlines the second kind of historical time she uses, "faraway history: events in the Balkans in 1945, in the West Indies in 1907, in India in 1857. All these summon up the consequences of grand historical events: war, earthquake, and mutiny, distantly, perhaps invisibly, shaping the lives of Smith's characters."

For example, when Samad is resisting the pull of Poppy Burt-Jones, he confides in Shiva, the handsome waiter at the Palace Restaurant. Shiva remarks, "I been out with a lot of white birds... but never with an English girl. Never works. Never." When Samad asks why not, Shiva answers, "Too much history.... Too much bloody history." And after Samad has broken off the affair, Shiva says again, "No, man, history, history. It's all brown man leaving English woman, it's all Nehru saying See-Ya to Madam Britannia."

For history and race cannot be divided in *White Teeth*. The history of British colonialism is written on the bodies of the characters, from Hortense Bowden, a product of interracial rape who disowns her own daughter for marrying a white man, to Samad Iqbal, who is obsessed with his ancestor Mangal Pande, a man he considers a hero despite the fact that "pandy" has become a British slang term for "coward." The Chalfens come to represent all that is laughable in the English middle classes, although they are actually middle-European Jews who fled racist genocide two generations back, while Millat, whose greatest dream is to be an Italian American gangster, settles for thuggish Islamic rebellion against an author whose works he has never read. Each of the characters is at the mercy not only of history but of their own mistaken analysis of the meaning of that history.

This comes to a head, of course, in the book's ending, where recent and faraway history come into collision as Samad Iqbal, in recognizing Marcus Chalfen's mentor as the doctor he thought Archie had killed back in the Balkans during World War II, is forced to reassess their fifty years of friendship. Even as Archie lunges to save Dr. Perret for a second time, taking another bullet in the leg as he does so, Samad experiences anagnorisis, a sudden realization of the formerly misapprehended truth of a situation. History, it seems, even recent history, is not written in stone, it is not the sort of truth that Samad hopes to find in Islam, but it is an ongoing story in which events continue to unfold.

Purity

Racial and religious purity are themes throughout the novel. While some characters, like Archie, are free of both religious longing and racial consciousness, most of the others are, to some extent, obsessed with the purity of their familial, racial, and religious heritage.

It is Alsana who sums up the impossibility of maintaining racial purity. After Samad sends Magid back to Bangladesh in order to protect his religious and ethnic identity, she and Samad argue one night. Brandishing the encyclopedia entry on Bengal, which notes that the Bengali people are descended from Indo-Aryans, Alsana berates Samad. "It just goes to show," she says, "you go back and back and it's still easier to find the correct Hoover bag than to find one pure person, one pure faith, on the globe."

While Magid disappoints his father by returning from Bangladesh an atheist and a "pukka Englishman," Millat responds to the confusion of multicultural London by diving into radical Islam, not out of a true desire for religious purity, but out of a longing for the purity of purpose he finds in gangster movies. Millat's devotion to KEVIN stems from his anger and from his determination that "if the game was God, if the game was a fight against the West, against the presumptions of Western science, against his brother or Marcus Chalfen, he was determined to win it."

Smith presents a variety of characters who believe that purity is possible, whether it is purity of religious belief, or purity of race, or purity of ethnic identity. And then to demonstrate the folly of this belief in purity, Smith pushes each one of them to the outermost comic boundary of what it might mean to live a pure life, and shows how they must fail, since perfect purity is impossible in the actual world.

Multiculturalism

Multiculturalism is the belief that minority cultures have intrinsic values, respect for which enriches all members of society. In the United States, the old notion was that the nation of immigrants was a "melting pot" in which ethnic identities would be subsumed into a homogenous new national identity. The metaphor multiculturalists prefer is the "salad bowl," in which ethnicities, like the separate ingredients in a salad, maintain their unique identities but come together to form a single dish.

One of the things that made *White Teeth* appear so new when it was published was the manner in which Smith uses multiple characters to give voice to the immigrant's fear of assimilation. In chapter 12, Smith's narrator notes that "it makes an immigrant laugh to hear the fears of the nationalist, scared of infection, penetration, miscegenation, when this is small fry, *peanuts*, compared to what the immigrant fears—dissolution, *disappearance*." This is what all of the immigrant parents fear for their children and the reason that Clara and Alsana find the entrance of their children into the Chalfens' world so threatening. And their concerns are not unfounded. In the same chapter, Irie admits that she rarely speaks about the Chalfens to her parents because she knows her mother worries, but nonetheless, she cannot control her "nebulous fifteen-year-old's passion for them, overwhelming, yet with no real direction or object. She just wanted to, well, kind of, *merge* with them. She wanted their Englishness."

The idea of maintaining cultural boundaries is tightly tied to the two other major themes of the novel, history and purity. Samad, overwhelmed with sorrow at how his sons have turned out, comes to visit Irie at her grandmother's house. Recounting how he came to England as a temporary measure, to make a little money, intending to go back, he tells her that he feels he has "made a devil's pact … it drags you in and suddenly you are unsuitable to return, your children are unrecognizable, you belong nowhere." Even worse, he continues, one begins to think that "the very *idea* of belonging … seems like some long, dirty lie." The irony is that to Irie, to the second-generation children, this "sounded like *paradise*.… Sounded like freedom."

And so, as many great novels do, *White Teeth* dramatizes the difficulties of life in a multicultural society. It does not propose solutions, it simply does what novels do best, builds characters whose lives give the reader some insight into what it is like to live in the world the author has created.

Postmodernism

Postmodernism is an imprecise term for a number of artistic and theoretical movements that have come into play in the wake of the modernist movement of the early twentieth century. Artists working in the modernist mode valued subjective experience and posited that one of the central values of art was to explore the core truth as experienced by coherent individuals. Postmodernists, influenced by thinkers like Jean Baudrillard, Roland Barthes, Michel Foucault, and others, reject the idea that individuals are self-creating in favor of the notion that individuals are a product of the eclectic and fragmentary political, social, and media forces with which they are continually bombarded. Postmodern fiction, then, tends to value fragmentation over coherence and favors the surface of the text over the notion that readers should identify with characters and their situations.

In her essay "Two Directions for the Novel," published in *Changing My Mind*, Smith gives a very short history of the postmodern literary project in a few sentences. She traces the long tradition of critique of the "nineteenth-century lyrical realism of Balzac and Flaubert" from "what Robbe-Grillet called 'the destitution of the old myths of depth'" through "a phenomenology skeptical of realism's metaphysical tendencies"; these critiques "peaked in that radical deconstructive doubt that questions the capacity of language itself to describe the world in any accuracy." The result is a sort of standoff between postmodernists and those who believe that fiction should express "the essential fullness and continuity of the self" by stressing the "transcendent importance of form" and "the incantatory power of language." What Smith, like those contemporary writers who reject this vision of literary merit, seeks to express and value as fully valid is a worldview that rejects "the secret, authentic heart of things." This aesthetic values "a rigorous attention to the damaged and the partial, the absent and the unspeakable."

In *White Teeth*, the postmodernist aesthetic is expressed in part through the novel's insistently comic tone. Events are played for laughs, from Archie's near suicide that opens the novel, to Hortense's riding in Ryan Topps's sidecar, to the ridiculous acronyms for the radical groups KEVIN and FATE. One way to focus the reader's attention on the surface of the text is to stress the ridiculous. Another hallmark of postmodern storytelling that Smith uses in *White Teeth* is the manner in which she uses pop-cultural referents, including movies, music, and clothing, as a means to fix character. Although Samad desperately wants his sons to define their lives by what he sees as the fixed and eternal truths of Islam, they define themselves instead by the fleeting values of late-capitalist society: music, clothing, movies, and political affiliations.

Point of View: Omniscient Third Person

White Teeth is written in the third person, a narrative stance in which the story is told not through the consciousness of a character but by a narrator who stands "outside" the narrative. Thus, this narrator is called a "third-person" narrator. Third-person narration is distinguished by the use of *he, she,* and *they* as pronouns rather than the first-person pronoun I or the second-person pronoun you. Third-person narrators are further divided into two types, limited and omniscient. In *White Teeth*, Smith uses a third-person omniscient or all-knowing narrator, that is, a narrator who knows more about the story than the characters do.

Third-person omniscient is the most common form of narration. It was largely rejected by the modernists because of the manner in which the omniscient narrator in novels of the eighteenth and nineteenth centuries tended to interrupt the narrative with commentary. This narrative stance posits a consciousness outside the action of the story; having access to the inner lives and thoughts of all the characters, it allows the author to break into the story in order to explain events and motivations to the reader. This seemed unrealistic to modernists, since many of them sought to replicate the stream-of-consciousness that they believed most closely represented lived experience.

Postmodernists, on the other hand, have taken to this narrative stance in part because it is "unrealistic." Since postmodernist novelists tend to resist the idea that reality can be represented in fiction, using the third-person omniscient narrator allows them to interrupt the text to remind the reader that what they have in their hands is a made object, not a reflection of reality. Postmodernists use the third-person omniscient narrator in a metafictional way, as a means of reminding the reader that the novel is a made-up story and that the characters, no matter how much one might identify with them, are not real people but were created by the author to act out the story, almost as if they were puppets.

In *White Teeth*, Smith uses the narrator to distance the reader from a sense that related events are real, to reinforce the fictionality of the novel. For instance, at the beginning of the second chapter, when the narrator states that "it's about time people told the truth about beautiful women. They do not shimmer down staircases. They do not descend, as was once supposed, from on high, attached to nothing other than wings." Here the narrator is puncturing exactly the romantic moment she set up in the previous chapter, when Archie felt time stop as Clara descended the stairs. The novel here announces its antiromantic stance via the narrator, who reveals herself as the one who is driving the narrative. And yet, Smith also uses the narrator in more traditional ways, to tell the reader what the characters are feeling, to fill in their backstories, to let the reader into their heads.

It was in large part because of the way she

combined traditional and postmodern storytelling that the book was such a success. Although it is clearly comic and intended to send up modern multicultural London, the characters have sufficient interiority, and the storytelling is satisfying enough in traditional ways to appeal to ordinary readers.

While *White Teeth* presents a portrait of modern multicultural London, its characters are obsessed with history, and events like the Indian Mutiny of 1857, the planter experience in Jamaica, World War II, and the end of the British Empire are crucial to understanding the story. An author of a review in the London *Guardian*, "In a Strange Land," notes that "this is also a novel of ideas, which tracks … the ineluctability of the past and of cultural and racial hybridity." The reviewer points out that Smith accomplishes this through circular storytelling, moving from Samad's investment in his great-grandfather, Mangal Pande, to using "the ubiquity of fag-ends in a north London school [to trigger] a disquisition on the English tobacco planter who impregnated Clara's grandmother."

Indian Mutiny of 1857

The core historical event in Samad Iqbal's personal time line is the Indian Mutiny of 1857—the Sepoy Rebellion—an event set off when his great-grandfather Mangal Pande (an actual historical figure borrowed by Smith) fired on his British commanding officer. Smith's account in the novel is historically accurate, recounting how Pande attacked the officers, was subdued, and was hanged several days later. The precipitating event of the mutiny was that the East India Company, which ruled India at the time, had switched to a military cartridge that had to be torn with the teeth. It was greased with animal fat that was rumored to be either lard (anathema to Muslims, who do not eat pork) or beef tallow (anathema to Hindus, to whom cattle are sacred). While Mangal Pande set off the mutiny, making him a hero to Samad Iqbal, his name became historical shorthand for "coward." While the mutiny did not ultimately succeed in wresting control of India away from the British Empire, it did end government of the colony by the East India Company. Company rule was replaced by a viceroy who was appointed by the Crown, an arrangement that lasted for the remaining ninety years of British rule.

British Immigration Policy Post–World War II

Before World War II, England was primarily a homogenous and ethnically white society. The end of the war left the nation physically destroyed by German bombing and with very little money for rebuilding. As the British Empire evolved into the Commonwealth, in which each nation has sovereignty over its own citizens, borders, and laws, a new citizenship status was created: "Citizen of the United Kingdom and Colonies." This status entitled any citizen of the Commonwealth to immigrate to England legally and to set up permanent residence. The labor shortage in England made immigration attractive, and former colonists from the Caribbean,

India, Pakistan, and African colonies began to move in large numbers. This was something of a shock to older Britons who were not accustomed to living among people of color or among large populations of Muslims and Hindus.

By the 1960s, concern over nonwhite immigration led to the passage of the Commonwealth Immigrants Acts of 1962 and 1968, which defined and limited the "right to abode." Nonetheless, globalization and multiculturalism have become the norm in England, as in most of the rest of the world, resulting in the establishment of mixed-race areas like Willesden Green, where *White Teeth* is set, as well as mixed-race families like the Joneses.

The Satanic Verses and the Fatwa against Salman Rushdie

In 1988 Salman Rushdie published his third novel, *The Satanic Verses*, an ironic, satirical story of two Indian Muslims who survive the destruction of their airplane by a terrorist bomb. The novel was an influence on Smith, especially for it's manic, magical-realist portrait of London's multicultural society. However, what *The Satanic Verses* is most remembered for is the fatwa, or Islamic decree, of death placed on Rushdie for ostensibly slandering Islam by the Islamic leader of Iran, Ayatollah Khomeini. Rushdie was taken into protective custody by the British government and lived in hiding for several years. Although he attempted to apologize, it made no difference, as the threat was primarily an exercise in political power. In a retrospective article published in the London *Guardian*, Andrew Anthony pointed out that despite Rushdie's several apologies and his claims to have reformed and to have taken up Islam again, the ayatollah said that it did not matter if Rushdie "became the most pious man of all time," it was still incumbent upon every Muslim to "employ everything he has got" to kill him. Bookstores were bombed, and several of his translators were killed, as was the Norwegian publisher of the novel. Bookstores pulled it from the shelves, and Rushdie continued to live under a heavy security presence. The novel and its protests appear in *White Teeth*; although unnamed, it is clearly a protest against that book to which Millat and his crew travel in 1989. The boys admit to not having read the book and to not even knowing anything about the author, but they vow to kill him anyhow. While the fatwa technically still remains in place, the Iranian government rescinded its backing in 1999. Rushdie has gone on to write several more novels and no longer lives in hiding.

However, as Anthony notes in his retrospective article in the *Guardian*, the fatwa has left a lasting legacy of censorship:

> Who would dare to write a book like *The Satanic Verses* nowadays? And if some brave or reckless author did dare, who would publish it? ... Any sentence might turn out to be a death

sentence. And few if any of even the boldest and most iconoclastic artists wish to run that risk.

History in *White Teeth* is always personal, retold in the stories of the various characters' experiences of wars, earthquakes, colonialism, immigration, and assimilation. It plays out in the actual lives of the characters and continues to influence their actions long after the seminal events have passed. In this, it forms one of the central themes of the book.

Critical Overview

Critical acclaim for *White Teeth* began even before the book's publication. Smith sent the first one hundred pages to the prestigious literary agent Andrew Wylie, and as the manuscript circulated through British publishing houses, excitement grew, leading to a heated auction for the publication rights. The book was an immediate bestseller in England. The novelist Caryl Phillips, writing in the London *Guardian*, called it "an audaciously assured contribution to this process of staring into the mirror. Her narrator is deeply self-conscious, so much so that one can almost hear the crisp echo of Salman Rushdie's footsteps." Phillips, an accomplished novelist himself, closed the review by claiming that Smith's

> wit, her breadth of vision and her ambition are of her own making. The plot is rich, at times dizzyingly so, but *White Teeth* squares up to the two questions which gnaw at the very roots of our modern condition: Who are we? Why are we here?

Later, on January 22, 2000, a second reviewer in the London *Guardian* noted of the book,

> scathingly irreverent without being flippant, engaged yet amused, its buoyant optimism perhaps reflects the fact that its author was born only

in the late 1970s, a child of a more relaxed racial climate than that of her literary forebears.

Referring to Smith's mixed-race background as well as to the novel's themes of race and fate, the reviewer closes the review by noting that "Its final image is the escape of a small brown laboratory mouse, which may be genetically programmed to turn albino-white, but which gladly seizes its freedom and runs with it."

Smith's reception in the United States was also enthusiastic. Michiko Kakutani, the *New York Times's* exacting lead critic, claims that *White Teeth* is

> a novel that announces the debut of a preternaturally gifted new writer—a writer who at the age of 24 demonstrates both an instinctive storytelling talent and a fully fashioned voice that's street-smart and learned, sassy and philosophical all at the same time.

Kakutani continues by noting that *White Teeth* announces, "This is someone who can do comedy, drama and satire, and do them all with exceptional confidence and brio."

Meanwhile, in *Salon*, Maria Russo noted the extraliterary attention the book garnered for Smith's youth, good looks, multiracial background, and class mobility. After all, she was a twenty-four-year-old biracial graduate of one of England's oldest and most prestigious universities who grew up in a housing estate in the immigrant working-class suburb of Willesden Green. Among the book's points of appeal, Russo notes, is that it "differs from many of its peers by not seeming to be motivated by a desire to express to the world how hard it is for her, or someone like her, to function." Russo also quotes Smith's own, unsigned review of her book in the short-lived British online literary magazine *Butterfly*. Instead of arguing with her critics, Smith seems to agree with them:

> This kind of precocity in so young a writer has one half of the audience standing to applaud and the other half wishing … she would just stay still and shut up. *White Teeth* is the literary equivalent of a hyperactive, ginger-haired tap-dancing 10-year-old.

While most critics have praised the novel for its inventive storytelling, vivid characters, and refreshing energy, James Wood calls these very qualities into question in an essay published in the *New Republic* in September 2001. He notes that "a genre is hardening" and that it is becoming possible to recognize the "contemporary idea of the 'big ambitious novel'" in part merely by the very energy for which *White Teeth* has been praised. This new genre, Wood claims, is

> a perpetual-motion machine that appears to have been embarrassed into velocity. It seems to want to

> abolish stillness, as if ashamed of Silence…. Inseparable from this culture of permanent storytelling is the pursuit of vitality at all costs. Indeed, vitality *is* storytelling, as far as these books are concerned.

He named this new genre "hysterical realism," a term that entered the lexicon of literary criticism and continues to be debated to this day. Perhaps best reflecting its merits, *White Teeth* was an international bestseller and won the Whitbread First Novel Award, the London *Guardian's* First Book Award, the James Tait Black Memorial Prize for Fiction, and the Commonwealth Writers' First Book Award.

What Do I Read Next?

- American Indian poet and novelist Sherman Alexie's first foray into young-adult fiction, *The Absolutely*

True Diary of a Part-Time Indian (2007), like *White Teeth* addresses issues of race, class, and clan. The story tells of Arnold Spirit (Junior), born with water on the brain, who is very bright and loves to draw. Along with his geeky looks, his habits makes him the target of bullies. When he transfers from the reservation school to a rich, white school, he expects the worst but finds, to his surprise, that he makes friends and even winds up on the basketball team. A game played against his old school causes Arnold to grapple with the meanings of tribe and community, even as he struggles to survive the deaths of several of his loved ones.

- One of the criticisms aimed at Smith when *White Teeth* was published was that her characters were "flat" and unbelievable. Taking on the question of just what makes a character, Smith chose twenty-two other authors and asked them one question: "make someone up." The result is the anthology *The Book of Other People* (2007), edited by Smith. It is a compendium of stories that address the very idea of character itself. Contributors include a who's who of contemporary fiction, including David Mitchell, Z. Z. Packer, Dave Eggers, Edwidge Danticat, and others.

- *On Beauty* (2006) is Smith's third novel and won the Orange Prize for Fiction. Set in Boston, it is the story of a mixed-race family of academics and is Smith's attempt to rework E. M. Forster's great *Howard's End* for the modern era. In this rich, multilayered novel, two families collide, the warm, open, multiracial Belseys and the uptight, Christian, conservative Kipps. The fathers of each clan are rival Rembrandt scholars who are forced to contend with Forster's famous dictum "only connect."

- Salman Rushdie's The *Satanic Verses* (1989) is probably the book Smith had in mind when Millat travels to Brixton to protest in *White Teeth*. One of the first novels to give voice to the multiplicity of identity experienced by English immigrants from the subcontinent, the novel's examination of good and evil is embedded in a feast of language served up by a writer at the height of his powers who takes on serious subjects in this rollicking comic fable. Clearly an influence on Smith,

Rushdie's novel was subsumed in the political furor it engendered, including a sustained death threat on Rushdie.

- Ryan Inzana's graphic novel *Johnny Jihad* (2003) opens as John Sendel of Trenton, New Jersey, speaks his last words into a tape recorder while being bombed by American forces in Afghanistan. Recruited as an aimless suburban teenager with a distant mother and a father who is both abusive and ex-military, *Johnny Jihad* follows Sendel as he finds purpose in life in the post-9/11 teachings of an anti-American imam. Like *White Teeth*, this graphic novel for young adults demonstrates how religious zealotry can both provide a sense of purpose and meaning to alienated young people and also pose great danger.

- Randa Abdel-Fatteh's hilarious and touching young-adult novel *Does My Head Look Big in This?* (2008) follows an Australian eleventh-grader named Ama who decides to wear the hijab, or head covering, fulltime. The story tells of her emotional and spiritual struggles as she copes with a mad crush on a boy, befriends an elderly Greek neighbor, and tries to help a friend who aspires to be a lawyer but whose well-intentioned mother is trying to force her to leave school and get married.

———————————————

Sources

Anthony, Andrew, "How One Book Ignited a Culture War," *in Guardian* (London, England), January 11, 2009, http://www.guardian.co.uk/books/2009/jan/11/salmanrushdie-satanic-verses?INTCMP=SRCH (accessed September 1, 2011).

"In a Strange Land, Zadie Smith's *White Teeth* Reveals a Major New Talent," in *Guardian* (London, England), January 22, 2000, http://www.guardian.co.uk/books/2000/jan/22/fictior (accessed September 1, 2011).

"Interview with Zadie Smith," in *BoldType*, http://www.randomhouse.com/boldtype/0700/smith/ (accessed September 1, 2011).

Kakutani, Michiko, "Books of the Times: Quirky, Sassy and Wise in a London of Exiles," in *New York Times*, April 25, 2000, http://www.nytimes.com/2000/04/25/books/books-of-the-times-quirky-sassy-and-wise-in-a-london-of-exiles.htmll (accessed September 1, 2011).

Lyall, Sarah, "Arts Abroad: Planning to Remain Anonymous, Thank You," in *New York Times*, December 17, 2002, http://www.nytimes.com/2002/12/17/books/arts-abroad-planning-to-remain-anonymous-thank-you.html?pagewanted=all (accessed September 1, 2011).

Mullan, John, "*Guardian* Book Club, Past Imperfect," in *Guardian* (London, England), October 5, 2002, http://www.guardian.co.uk/books/2002/oct/05/za INTCMP=SRCH (accessed September 1, 2011).

Phillips, Caryl, "Mixed and Matched," Review of *White Teeth*, in *Guardian* (London, England), January 9, 2000, http://www.guardian.co.uk/books/2000/jan/09/fiction (accessed September 1, 2011).

Russo, Maria, "Girl Wonder," in *Salon*, April 28, 2000, http://www.salon.com/books/feature/2000/04/28/zad (accessed September 1, 2011).

Smith, Zadie, *Changing My Mind*, Penguin, 2009, pp. 74, 94.

——, "This Is How It Feels to Me," in Guardian (London, England), October 13, 2001, http://www.guardian.co.uk/books/2001/oct/13/fiction INTCMP=SRCH (accessed September 1, 2011).

——, *White Teeth*, Random House, 2000.

Wood, James, "Human, All Too Inhuman," *in New Republic*, August 20, 2001, http://www.powells.com/review/2001_08_30.html (accessed September 1, 2011).

Further Reading

Ali, Monica, *Brick Lane*, Scribner, 2003.

> Set in Brick Lane, an actual neighborhood of London, Ali's first novel is the story of Nanzeen, whose parents arrange her marriage to Chanu, an educated but ineffective man twenty years her senior. He takes her to London, where she sews clothing by the piece and raises two children. This unsentimental tale of one woman's coming into adulthood is also a perceptive portrait of London's East Indian community.

Eggers, Dave, A *Heartbreaking Work of Staggering Genius*, Simon & Schuster, 2000.

> When Dave Eggers was twenty-two, his parents died of cancer in short succession, leaving him and his sister to raise his seven-year-old brother. They moved to San Francisco, where Eggers simultaneously started writing for independent magazines and became a very young single parent. Written in a manic allusive style, this is one of the books that, like *White Teeth*, set the tone for writing in the early part of the 2000s.

Franzen, Jonathan, *How to Be Alone: Essays*, Farrar, Straus, and Giroux, 2002.

> Franzen is one of the novelists most often mentioned in concert with Smith and Wallace, and in this collection of essays he sets out the key artistic challenges that he believes writers of his generation face. He addresses topics ranging from a long discussion of why the novel still matters, to a meditation on how Alzheimer's affects his father's brain, to an essay on the nature and value of "difficult" fiction. Several of these essays won awards when first published as magazine articles.

Levy, Andrea, *Small Island*, St. Martin's Press, 2004.

> Levy's novel follows two families, one Jamaican and one English, in the aftermath of World War II. Gilbert and Hortense immigrate from Jamaica to England, taking a room in Queenie's house. When her husband, Bernard, finally returns home from the war, he is not pleased to find black immigrants living there. The novel unfolds over several decades and is told from each character's point of view, dramatizing the many upheavals that immigration brought to the country.

Wallace, David Foster, *Brief Interviews with Hideous Men*, Little, Brown, 1999.

> This book was a huge influence on Smith, and she has an extensive essay in *Changing My Mind* about the collection and the impact David Foster Wallace had on modern fiction. The volume is a collection of twenty-three short stories, many of which are cast as interviews in which the interviewer's questions are omitted. Wallace's fiction demonstrates all the difficulties of postmodern fiction—the narrative thread can be difficult to follow, and the footnotes can be distracting—but there is no discounting the power of his prose or his influence on writers of his generation.

Wood, James, The *Irresponsible Self: On Laughter and the Novel*, Farrar, Straus, and Giroux, 2004.

> Literary critic James Wood coined the term "hysterical realism" for the sort of writing that Smith, Eggers, Wallace, and others were beginning to publish at the turn of the twenty-first century. The essay in which he outlines this concept appears in this collection along with twenty-two other essays on the ways that laughter and comedy function in the novel.

Suggested Search Terms

Zadie Smith

Zadie Smith AND White Teeth

Zadie Smith AND multiculturalism

hysterical realism

Zadie Smith AND postmodernism

Zadie Smith AND interview

Zadie Smith AND biography

postcolonial fiction

black fiction AND Britain

immigration AND fiction

Printed in October 2021
by Rotomail Italia S.p.A., Vignate (MI) - Italy